The American Century Series

TINTON FALLS
IN THE TWENTIETH CENTURY

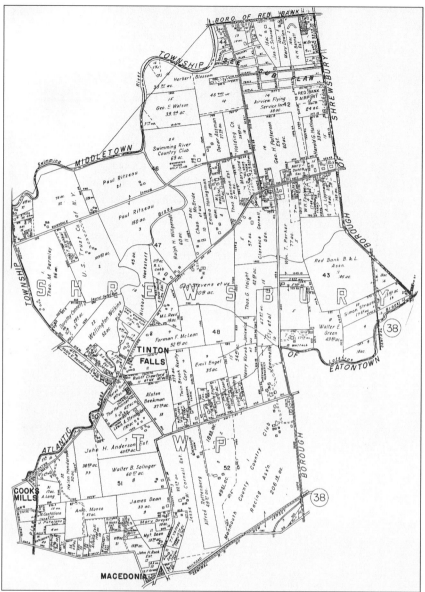

Tinton Falls, north of the railroad, a traditional divide of the borough's northern and southern sections, is seen on the 1941 Franklin Survey Company map, labeled Shrewsbury Township. A portion of the Red Bank Building and Loan Association tract (right), bordering on Shrewsbury Avenue, the borough's eastern boundary at that section, was bought by the federal government and developed as Vail Homes, and today is the only remaining part of the township. The Garden State Parkway bisected the borough in 1953. Overpasses were built on two of the three east-west roads depicted here, Sycamore and Tinton Avenues, but the northernmost one, Riverdale Avenue, was cut in two. The Parkway's opening in 1954 led to a borough population boom. The Monmouth County Country Club at bottom right is now part of the Charles Wood area of Fort Monmouth. Two no-longer-extant facilities once identified with Red Bank are seen in the northeast, the airport on Shrewsbury Avenue and the baseball stadium on Newman Springs Road.

THE AMERICAN CENTURY SERIES

TINTON FALLS

IN THE TWENTIETH CENTURY

Randall Gabrielan

ARCADIA

Copyright © 1999 by Randall Gabrielan.
ISBN 0-7524-0822-4

Published by Arcadia Publishing,
an imprint of Tempus Publishing, Inc.
2 Cumberland Street
Charleston, SC 29401

Printed in Great Britain.

Library of Congress Catalog Card Number: 99-61643

For all general information contact Arcadia Publishing at:
Telephone 843-853-2070
Fax 843-853-0044
E-Mail arcadia@charleston.net

For customer service and orders:
Toll-Free 1-888-313-BOOK

Visit us on the internet at http://www.arcadiaimages.com

This book is dedicated to Jamie Carter, my editor at Arcadia for the past two years. She is cherished for her warmth, cheerfulness, and good humor, along with the ability to guide the author with gentle encouragement. As she expands her career goals, I shall remember her time at Arcadia fondly, for the expansion of the company, our roles with it, and the joy of a fine, close, working relationship.

Cover photograph: Marjorie Clarahan is crowned Miss New Shrewsbury at the 1974 fair. Placing the crown is Kim MacCallum, the 1973 winner. The three first runners-up are Joan Ervin (on the rear of the cover) and, to the winner's left, Jill Brown and Laura Ridner.

4

CONTENTS

Acknowledgments   6

Introduction   7

1.   A Stream, Its Mills, and Bridge   9

2.   Houses and Farms   21

3.   Business   57

4.   Schools   71

5.   Organizations   83

6.   People, Places, and Events   111

ACKNOWLEDGMENTS

The generous contributions of many picture lenders made this work possible. I am especially indebted to several present or former borough residents. Wilma Crawford O'Callaghan's numerous, fine pictures reflected well the generations her family has lived in Tinton Falls village. Robert Stanley Osborn's photographing the village in 1952 for a college project provided a now-dated glimpse of a settlement that has changed markedly in his lifetime. Richard C. Winters provided old pictures of special significance and beauty. Mildred Taylor and Clare Thomas Garland offered insight and images of the African-American communities, Clare's including the Native Americans who intermarried with Monmouth County blacks. Residents Bill and Bea Anderson were helpful with the border neighborhood of Wayside, as was collector Glenn Vogel. Dorothy Stevens Roberts' father George, a former mayor, died during the project. I thank her for contributing memories of him, a stalwart of the borough movement. Fort Monmouth is divided among three municipalities. The Tinton Falls segment is well represented thanks to Richard Bingham, Ph.D., Command Historian, United States Army Communications-Electronics Command.

Thanks to all the lenders of photographs, my co-producers, including Blake Banta of Curvon Corp., Olga Boeckel, Ruth G. Borden, Moe Cuocci, Michael Brady of the Earle Naval Weapons Station, Mindy Rosewitz of the Electronics-Communications Museum of Fort Monmouth, Stephen Grabley, William Edmund Kemble, Evelyn Leavens, John Lentz, Susan Martin, Monroe Marx, Gail Hunton of the Monmouth County Parks System, Ruthanne Morford, Ole Palludin, Daniel Patalano, Melinda Goray McAleer of Ranney School, Special Collections & Archives of Rutgers University Libraries, Robert A. Schoeffling, the Shrewsbury Historical Society, the late Charles Toop, and Katherine C. Welch. Thanks, too, to the Reverend Alan Schaefer of the Hope Presbyterian Church and Elder Kenneth Noland of the Monmouth County Church of Christ for substantive material on their churches.

INTRODUCTION

The Borough of Tinton Falls is a historic paradox. At its core is a 17th-century settlement, but the municipality's make-up was shaped by the 20th century and its corporate existence was created only in 1950. Tinton Falls, the practical remainder of once-vast Shrewsbury Township, is not only a product of our times, but its history can be neatly quartered with the present century.

The modern history of Shrewsbury Township, founded in 1693, may be said to begin in 1849 with the separation of Ocean Township. The 1840s was a decade when most "original" townships in New Jersey were divided into parts to become administratively manageable by the standards of those times. Shrewsbury Township lost Eatontown in 1873, but stayed largely intact until the first quarter of the 20th century, when it was fragmented by the borough government movement. New Jersey, motivated by strong home-rule inclinations, had laws that made forming new municipal "homes" easy and inexpensive.

Boroughs organized from Shrewsbury Township during the first quarter of the 20th century include Rumson (1907), Red Bank (1908, although it had been a town within the township since 1870), Fair Haven (1912), and Little Silver (1923). These places were the growing areas of the Red Bank-Rumson peninsula between the Navesink and Shrewsbury Rivers; the township was left with its oldest historic settlement, Shrewsbury Village, and its rural inland parts.

Economy of municipal operation was one motivation to organize boroughs into smaller, compact entities that could be administered for less money in those times. The author examined a documentary example prior to publication by comparing 1911 Shrewsbury Township and 1912 Borough of Fair Haven tax bills for the same Fair Haven tract. Property taxes were small then by present standards, but the percentage difference was noteworthy. The increased burdens on the rural remainder were expected and protested by John Applegate, Shrewsbury Township's counsel in opposing Fair Haven's separation.

The Borough of Shrewsbury's separation in 1926 was motivated in large part by zoning, as the historic center of Shrewsbury Village had become a "millionaire's row." Its influential citizens wished to keep distant from small-lot, inexpensive house developments such as Hance Park in present Tinton Falls, or similar subdivisions that were sprouting in Red Bank.

Rural Shrewsbury Township became the site of a government housing development (p. 127) that was expected to be temporary. However, Vail Homes' permanence became apparent after World War II, and nearly doubled the township's residents, populating it with government renters who did not pay real estate taxes. They had, however, an equal voice in raising and expending taxes, and promised to re-shape the municipality according to their wishes.

The remainder of the township responded by seeking separate municipal organization. Lawyers Lawrence A. Carton Jr. and Howard W. Roberts lobbied assiduously at the federal, state, and county levels to secure political approval. The latter was one of the most powerful figures in Monmouth County, while Judge Carton, who drafted the legal work and continued representation of the borough after separation, may be considered the "father of the borough of Tinton Falls."

The separatists first proposed the name Old Shrewsbury to reflect the town's ancient roots, but it brought strong objection from the Borough of Shrewsbury. A 266 to 174 majority adopted New Shrewsbury as a compromise, the name under which a local referendum approved the separation in July 1950. The federal government sold Vail Homes to a cooperative organization in 1957. That housing development is today's Shrewsbury Township, the heir to a three-century municipal corporation.

The 1954 opening of the Garden State Parkway physically split the borough and sparked growth, which, subject to periodic fluctuation, continues unabated. The old rural township lacked recognizable identity as it consisted of several named localities, received its mail from various post offices, and contained areas on its borders often indistinguishable from nearby towns. The name New Shrewsbury did little to establish identity; it actually confused people. The new borough changed its name in 1975 (p. 97), adopting that of its oldest locality, which readily distinguished it from Shrewsbury Township and the Borough of Shrewsbury. A new insignia helped spark recognition, but the concurrent goal of establishing municipal-wide postal identity was elusive. A plan to establish a Tinton Falls post office was announced in 1998, although its establishment will take time.

A 300-year-old locality provided the Tinton Falls name, the designation Lewis Morris gave to the early iron works he bought, expanded, and operated as the area's first industry and the origin of iron manufacture in New Jersey. Its omission from this book's pictorial body acknowledges that the lack of an available image necessitates a regrettable gap.

This work uses the three municipal names interchangeably at times. Shrewsbury Township and New Shrewsbury are specified in places where clarity dictates; however, Tinton Falls is used for ease of reference in some places where the picture pre-dates that borough name.

The telling of Tinton Falls' history has its omissions, notably from the once sparsely settled south. The author hopes the work may be continued, perhaps in a second volume, and looks forward to contact with those with pictures to lend for copying. His address and phone number are 71 Fish Hawk Drive, Middletown, New Jersey 07748, (732) 671-2645.

Tintern Abbey, built in the late 13th century in Monmouthshire, Wales, one of the United Kingdom's most charming ruins, is generally accepted as the origin of the name Tinton Falls.

One

A Stream, Its Mills, and Bridge

The Falls at Shrewsbury, the earlier name of Tinton Falls, was a major physical feature on the 1660s Monmouth County landscape. Located on the Hockhockson branch of the Swimming River, now known as Pine Brook, the ledge was formed by indurated, green earth, a material used as marl fertilizer, and a drop that was formerly 30 feet. This view of the falls is a c. 1905 postcard; the former sawmill is at right.

The waters below the falls contained a well-known mineral spring (opposite) "frequently visited by those who seek health or amusement at the boarding houses near the coast," according to Thomas Gordon's 1834 *Gazetteer of the State of New Jersey*. Barber and Howes' 1844 *Historical Collections of the State of New Jersey* noted, "the stream winds for some distance through a romantic dell overhung by trees of variegated foliage"; it is seen on a *c.* 1907 postcard, the exact locale not identified.

James Grover, an original patentee of the 1665 Monmouth Patent, owned an extensive tract at Tinton Falls. Iron recovery was made there *c.* 1670, and is the origin of New Jersey's iron industry. Considerable capital was needed for manufacturing the metal, a factor in the 1675 sale of 3,540 acres to Lewis Morris of Barbados. The dam above the falls facilitated waterpower for the forge's operation.

Tinton Falls Village contained a chalybeate spring, its water containing iron, copper, sulfur, etc. Local Native Americans, who reserved rights to its access after selling the land, held it in high repute. Barber and Howe indicated (1844), "When taken from the spring, [water] is clear, but on standing a few hours it assumes the color of cider and discolors glasses in which it is placed." Seen possibly *c.* 1930, the spring was enveloped by a brick wall, had its surface covered by yellowish hydrated iron oxide, and contained an outlet pipe (right). (Special Collections & Archives, Rutgers University Libraries.)

The destruction of the dam and erosion, which has continued into the present generation, have reduced the size of the falls considerably. The unidentified figures, perhaps Wallings, from the early years of this century, may suggest the falls' diminished size. (Collection of Richard C. Winters.)

A sawmill stood on the east side of Tinton Avenue, north of the bridge, and opposite the gristmill. The abandoned structure, owned by Daniel H. Cook, was photographed in July 1895 by Vernon D. Cook from the southwest corner of the bridge. (Collection of Robert S. Osborn.)

Peter S. Walling's sketch of the village shows the tollhouse on the east side of Tinton Avenue looking toward today's village green, then the site of the Mineral Springs Hotel. The front gabled structure at the left, rear, appears to be the early firehouse (p. 102). The 35-by-60-foot hotel, once an active center of village life, was reportedly built in two sections. The northern part, formerly a store, dated from the early 19th century. The southern part was added in the middle of that century. The hotel, having three rooms and a bar on the first floor and eight rooms plus a ballroom upstairs, was destroyed by fire in October 1916.

A gristmill has reportedly stood on the south bank of Pine Brook since the 1670s, but the age of the present building is unknown. Given the perilous existence of mill structures, which were often destroyed and rebuilt, and the mixed construction of this one, it probably dates from the early 19th century, and may have been erected on an older foundation. Old pictures of such a significant landmark are surprisingly rare. This one was taken from the village green c. 1939. (Photograph by W. Edmund Kemble.)

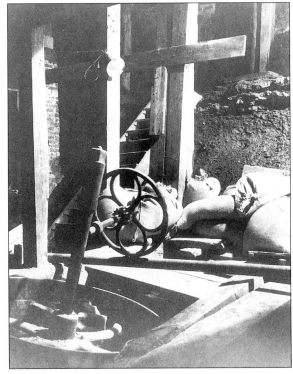

Milling ceased with Samuel J. Bennett's c. 1921 sale of the property. He had a 33-year career and was known as the "honest miller of Tinton Falls," having earned the reputation through hard work at a time when local milling was supplanted by large Midwestern milling centers. Grain sacks and equipment appear only recently abandoned, although this picture was taken in 1949. (Special Collection & Archives, Rutgers University Libraries.)

Four artists joined in 1950 to found the Old Mill Gallery at the former gristmill. They were Geza de Vegh, Commander J. Douglas Gessford, Thomas Frelinghuysen, and John Held Jr. Owner de Vegh was a force behind the later Old Mill Association, a not-for-profit organization that sought to turn the mill into a cultural center featuring music and theater. De Vegh is seen in his sculpture studio in the 1940s. (The Dorn's Collection.)

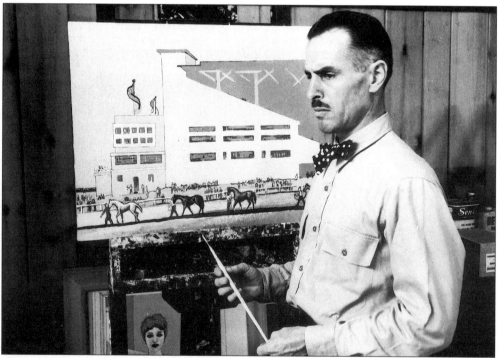

Geza de Vegh was born in Hungary in 1905, earned a law degree at the University of Budapest in 1929, studied art, and came to America in 1930. His early career as a sculptor's assistant included work on the facade of the Cathedral of St. John the Divine in New York City, among other notable buildings. He became a citizen in 1936 and took a career turn to industrial design of ceramics, glass, metal, and porcelain. He bought the mill in 1943, seeking an outlet for his ceramic plans. (The Dorn's Collection.)

14

The basement floors of the mill included de Vegh's ceramic studio and kilns. He is seen there with his wife, the former Virginia Armstrong, in 1949. Their specialty was the Toby Jug, which often incorporated New Jersey themes and characters. De Vegh also developed a popular line of utilitarian pottery, using a Perth Amboy factory for mass-market production. Virginia died in 1966 and Geza in 1989. (Special Collection & Archives, Rutgers University Libraries.)

Four large millstones, each with an estimated weight of 2,000 pounds, were removed in May 1956 from an upper level of the mill in order to reduce weight in the building and to provide more room. Stones wear out and the ages of these have not been determined, but they date, perhaps, from the second half of the 19th century. (The Dorn's Collection.)

Richard Edwards of Neptune is watching the downward progress of one stone. The mill was built on sloping ground. Only a small section of the foundation is visible on the south facade (p. 13), but the north shows four levels of basement on the creek side that are only partially visible here. (The Dorn's Collection.)

The old mill was the site of a dinner theater for 11 seasons, closing in the summer of 1986. Tom Frascatore is in character as Toulouse-Latrec, but looking more like Groucho Marx in a 1978 production of the comedy *El Grande De Coca Cola*. His romantic interest is a ballerina portrayed by Jane Milmore, seen as a pert profile in petulance. One reviewer claimed the zany play was like its namesake soft drink, refreshing but of little lasting value.

The falls can be readily viewed today from behind the mill structure, or from the parking lot to its east, as seen in this 1975 photograph. Erosion has lowered their drop considerably, a process that has continued over the past 40 years.

The small structure at right is the Tinton and Sycamore Avenues tollhouse (also on p. 12). Toll roads were unpopular in late-19th-century Monmouth County. An 1882 visitor, writing for the *Register* under the name "The Traveler," claimed, "Some of the farmers will travel a mile out of their way with a load to avoid paying two cents toll." He noted that local opposition was not as vigorous as at other Monmouth locales and the toll roads were kept in good condition, something that was, at the time, not always a benefit of toll paying. The mill is at the left in this view, which likely dates back to the late 19th century.

The *c.* 1900 Pratt Pony truss bridge spanning Pine Brook is seen on a *c.* 1905 postcard. (Collection of Glenn Vogel.)

Tinton Avenue is viewed looking north across the bridge *c.* 1890s. The building on the northwest corner of Water Street, long a bar and now a restaurant, was Vanderveer's grocery. The sawmill right of center was still active as the presence of logs indicates. The fence at left suggests the present gas station site was then still a house lot.

A signal light, located south of the bridge, now controls traffic; this view dates from 1952. The Coleman house (see p. 30) in the background was destroyed by fire in 1976. The pounding of modern traffic deteriorated the near century-old bridge, resulting in a weight limit reduction from 16 to 5 tons. Its replacement was planned around 1990. (The Dorn's Collection.)

A bridge and the business building to its west are constants in the northerly views of Tinton Avenue taken perhaps 70 years apart. Comparing this with the picture opposite reveals numerous minor and substantive changes at the village crossroads.

A Borough versus County dispute arose over the width and number of lanes of the replacement bridge, the issues embracing safety needs and the impact of a wider bridge on a district on the National Register of Historic Places. The County's initial proposal of a four-lane, 55-foot bridge inclusive of a pedestrian path was changed to a 46-foot cartway with a separate pedestrian bridge on the west side. The four lanes were retained. The old bridge was demolished in 1997. (Collection of Robert S. Osborn.)

The two western lanes of the new bridge, seen under construction in March 1997, were erected while the old bridge remained in service. Upon their completion, the old bridge was demolished and the two other lanes were built, an innovative process for a Monmouth County bridge. They were completed in September 1997. A fieldstone cladding disguises its concrete construction. The author believes the bridge represents a reasonable compromise of safety, aesthetics, and mitigated impact on a historic district. (Collection of Robert S. Osborn.)

Two

HOUSES AND FARMS

Frank Lawes Sr., husband of Florence, and his handsome steed are seen on an unidentified street, perhaps Riverdale Avenue, at the turn of the century. Frank died in 1933. (Collection Shrewsbury Historical Society.)

William Henry Lawes' Holly Farm was a riverfront resort/boarding house on Riverdale Avenue, earlier known as Lawes Bridge Road, with about 52 acres. It was later owned by Mrs. E.W. Chapin. This Charles Foxwell photograph is from the turn of the century. (Collection Shrewsbury Historical Society.)

Evan Jones, a Jersey City native, came to the Tinton Falls area around 1900. He is seen here with Gertrude T. Lawes Guptil c. 1910. He died in 1935. (Collection Shrewsbury Historical Society.)

An unidentified man is in front of Evan Jones' Riverdale Avenue house early in this century. The house was destroyed by fire in the early 1930s. (Collection Shrewsbury Historical Society.)

William Henry Lawes, a native of England, served as a Union Army druggist in the Civil War. He is seen, perhaps in the 1920s, with his daughter, Gertrude Tamlyn Lawes Guptil, and his granddaughter, Jane Tamlyn Guptil Powers. Lawes died in 1926. Gertrude, who was born on Holly Farm, survived until 1966. Jane donated the picture to its owner. (Collection Shrewsbury Historical Society.)

The house at 85 Swimming River Road was likely built *c.* 1865 when Harry Dibben purchased the surrounding farm. Harry's family held the property until 1913, when his heirs sold the house with 96 acres to Theodore Parmly, who maintained an orchard into modern times. The house, with Italianate and Greek Revival influence, shows little facade change, with the exception of the garage addition to the north.

Parmly, who is remembered by the name of Parmly Road, sold his orchard in the 1950s for the Stonehaven development of about 116 ranch houses built by Jayden Brothers. Dick Winters was behind either the wheel or lens for this picture of a tournadozer, a rubber tire bulldozer owned by the contractor Hess Brothers. Dick recalls the enclosed cab was well heated in winter. (Collection Richard C. Winters.)

Wellington Wilkins Sr. bought the John Johnson farm of 82 acres fronting on the east side of Swimming River Road in 1903, immediately making improvements to the outbuildings and adding a slate roof to the house. He farmed the place for about 14 years, then moved to a house in the village and sold the then-28.5-acre farm to Dorothy Connolly in 1935. She made various changes to the old house, part of which may date to the late 18th century, enlarging rooms, replacing the porch, and adding a four-room servants wing. This picture is from the Spring-Summer 1937 edition of the *Monmouth Pictorial*.

The Wellington Wilkins family is seen *c.* early 1950s, from left to right, as follows: (seated) Wellington Sr. and his wife, Caroline; (middle) Robin Wilkins, Winkie Wilkins, Gail Wilkins Sathmary, Wellington Jr., and his wife, Wilma, holding Karen; (rear) Jane Wilkins and Dr. Stanley Wilkins, a Red Bank physician. (Collection Robert S. Osborn.)

The Colonial Revival house at 400 Riverdale Avenue West was built on the former Wilkins farm, probably in the 1930s. It was home to Frank Weny, owner of Willowbrook Farms, known as the "Home of the Hobos," from 1972 until his death in 1998.

Weny built the track south of the house that for years was home of the Sire Stakes races. The Willowbrook Farms stable bred trotting horses, which were identifiable by the "Hobo" prefix in their names.

Born in 1832 in Keyport, David Augustus Walling left as a youth for New York, entering maritime service as a cabin boy, rising through the ranks while sailing the world. Captain Walling commanded a food ship in the Civil War, losing one vessel to capture by Confederates. He retired to mercantile pursuits, opening a store in the Belmar area, where he remained until his 1883 purchase of the Arthur Wilson distillery and cider mill in Tinton Falls. Walling married Sara Elizabeth Sherman in 1859; they had five children. He died in 1914.

The *c.* 1860s Italianate Arthur Wilson house at 771 Tinton Avenue is associated with two operators of the adjacent apple distillery, Wilson and David Walling. The little-changed house, seen in 1952 looking south toward the bridge, has attractive vergeboard on its gable ends. (Collection of Robert S. Osborn.)

John Henry Osborn built this Colonial Revival house at 811 Tinton Avenue in 1938. Labor was ample and skilled at the time, recalled son Bob, including masons who erected the handsome chimney from 15 tons of peanut stone hauled in small quantities from quarries in the Chapel Hill area of Middletown. The picture of the little-changed house dates from 1952. (Collection of Robert S. Osborn.)

Wellington Wilkins Sr. moved to this c.1860s house at 682 Tinton Avenue, seen in 1952, after retiring from farming. (Collection of Robert S. Osborn.)

The still-standing Four Square House at 803 Tinton Avenue is seen *c.* 1935 next to George Wentorff's gas station, located at the site of the low brick wall now on the premises. A service station on a residential street would be thankfully banned under typical contemporary zoning standards, something to remember when someone brings up the "intrusiveness" of government. The image is from a scarce Sun Oil Company advertising postcard.

De Camp Statler bought a lot spanning the Tinton Falls-Colts Neck border from Annie Wilkins, George's widow, in 1939. The little-changed ranch house, seen in 1952, is a typical late-1930s design, although it has not been ascertained if a wing was a later addition. (Collection of Robert S. Osborn.)

The *c.* early-19th-century house at 774 Tinton Avenue, seen in 1952, was owned for many years by the Hubbard family, which reportedly owned the property since the early 18th century. A one-story, end-gabled addition was later built on the north end (right). (Collection of Robert S. Osborn.)

The Coleman house at 750 Tinton Avenue, one of the oldest houses in the village, is shown here in 1952. It was destroyed by fire November 22, 1976, and its lot, adjacent to the bridge, is now vacant. (Collection of Robert S. Osborn.)

The Crawford house at 750 Tinton Avenue likely dates from the first half of the 19th century, with the parts at left probably latter additions. The picture dates from 1900, an easy inference as Ella Brower Crawford is holding Marion Crawford Conley Draycort, born that September. Cara Pearl Crawford Harrison is standing under her sister, while Allen E. Crawford is in front.

The Crawford house was given Colonial Revival modifications, perhaps near the time of this c. 1925 photograph. They included the construction of dormers and the addition of a porch, with the half at right later enclosed to serve as the municipal tax collection office. That change is virtually the only one visible today. Wilma O'Callaghan, lender of the picture, believes the second couple from the left is likely her parents, Allen and Ruth Crawford.

John C. Crawford, seen *c.* 1900, established a wholesale meat business in the village. He served as a member of the Red Bank cavalry troop and on the Shrewsbury Township Committee. Crawford married twice; his widow was the former Mary Jane Lennox of Scotland. He left two daughters and a son, Allen E.

Allen Eastmond Crawford, born *c.* 1898, retired in 1965 after 47 years in the family meat business. He served 21 years as tax collector for the township of Shrewsbury and was a charter member and ex-chief of the Tinton Falls Fire Company. Crawford, who was married to Ruth Brown Tilton, died in 1970.

Four of Allen and Ruth Crawford's children are seen on July 25, 1935. From left they are Ann, Allen Eastmond, Wilma Ellynore, and Joan. Wilma preserved the picture, as well as much family history, lending it for publication.

Ruth Brown Tilton, born 1905 in Marlboro, moved to Tinton Falls around 1920 and married Allen E. Crawford in 1924. Ruth served Tinton Falls and its predecessor Shrewsbury Township as tax collector and treasurer for 47 years, retiring in 1973. She is seen outside the borough hall near her retirement year. During the Depression, Ruth was known to have paid the taxes for more than one of her classmates. She was a member of the Wayside Methodist Church and many civic and fraternal organizations, serving the Tinton Falls Fire Company Ladies Auxiliary as treasurer. Ruth died in 1986.

Left: Cara Pearl Crawford was born in 1896 in the Crawford home (see p. 31). She married Leslie Harrison and became a practical nurse. *Right:* George O'Callaghan was a Navy veteran of World War II, having served as a ship's cook. He was also a chief of the Tinton Falls Fire Company No. 1, a captain of the Tinton Falls First Aid Squad, and a salesman for the Lawes Company in Shrewsbury for many years. He died in January 1997 at age 76. *Below:* George O'Callaghan's house, at 760 Tinton Avenue, was a 20th-century addition to the historic district landscape. (House—Collection of Robert S. Osborn.)

One of the oldest village houses, 755 Tinton Avenue, was built in two sections during the 18th century. The older section, standing over a crawl space, is attributed to 1716, while the addition, attributed to the late 18th century, is built on a stone foundation over a basement. Early on the property was owned by the Morris family; in the late 19th century, it was owned by J.P. Truax, a saw miller. The sawmill (p. 12) was adjacent on the south. This picture is dated 1952, prior to the addition of two dormers. (Collection of Robert S. Osborn.)

A blacksmith once occupied the barn adjacent on the north to 755 Tinton Avenue. Mrs. William A. Barrett, a recent owner, is seen in 1976 next to the brick forge attributed to Aaron Tilton, a 19th-century owner. A woodworking shop occupies the premises now.

The miller's house at 1213 Sycamore Avenue, of early-18th-century origin, was one of the oldest in the village. Located adjacent to the mill, its recent noteworthy owner was Geza de Vegh, former mill owner and artist. It was reported as a site of Revolutionary War activity and is seen in 1952, looking east on Sycamore Avenue. (Collection of Robert S. Osborn.)

A fire of unknown origin broke out in the early morning hours of June 5, 1977, destroying the miller's house. The owners, who also owned the adjacent restaurant at the mill, gave Len Bianchi a two-day period for an archeological search before the grounds were turned into a parking lot. He is seen on the site June 24, 1977, on a dig that revealed numerous old artifacts.

The house at 1171 Sycamore Avenue, once owned by Dr. Ernest Robinson and seen here in 1952, was in deteriorated condition prior to its demolition in the late 1980s for the new houses on Running Brook Drive. (Collection of Robert S. Osborn.)

The entrance to Twin Sycamore Farms on the north side of Sycamore Avenue was near Running Brook Drive.

In 1939, John Lemon bought 1181 Sycamore Avenue from Harry Coleman. He had earlier purchased Coleman's butcher business and operated a slaughterhouse in the rear of these premises. The rear porch is no longer enclosed, but the stucco-clad house still looks similar to the way it does in this 1952 picture.

The Twin Sycamore Rod & Gun Club was located on the north side of Sycamore Avenue east of the house on the bottom of p. 37. Sunday afternoon was the favored gunning time. One can hardly imagine a gun club in a now-developed part of town, but another still exists on Green Grove Road.

The Italianate house at 729 Sycamore Avenue was built in two sections beginning *c.* 1860 and was once located on the 351-acre George Hance farm.

The late-18th-century house at 755 Sycamore Avenue was bought by George Hance *c.* 1838 following his marriage to Sarah White of Shrewsbury.

The Greek Revival-style house at 904 Sycamore Avenue, likely built *c.* 1830–50 in two sections—the eastern part is older—was the seat of a 109-acre farm that was owned in the late 19th century by Jacob Shutts. After a brief and unsuccessful ownership by another in the late 1920s, the place was first rented and then bought in 1939 by George Stevens.

The Stevens family is seen in 1939 at the rear of the Sycamore Avenue house. George is surrounded by his three daughters, from the left, Dorothy, Barbara, and Marjorie. His wife, Muriel, completes the family portrait at a part of the house extensively damaged by fire in 1947.

George Stevens (1906–1998) had a knack for practical invention. He is seen with his gate opener, which had a rod attached to the pictured wheel and opened a gate when struck by a vehicle. A balance on the device closed it. Another device cultivated soil while dropping fertilizer.

Production on the Stevens farm varied over time. It was a vegetable farm in the early years, but later grew potatoes and hybrid seed corn. Stevens switched to dairy production, including grain and hay for the animals. He is seen third from the left, receiving from Frank Moreau an award for service to agriculture. At left are Andrew Conover, a lawyer, and Richard Applegate.

Stevens also raised pumpkins, with daughter Dorothy posing with some fine examples in a picture first published in the Autumn-Winter 1936 issue of the *Monmouth Pictorial*. Did they always toss around the pumpkins? Dorothy indicated no, but recalled they would play to the camera when a photo opportunity arose.

Sycamore Manor is representative of 1950s housing developments. This view of Knollwood Drive was taken from the lawn of the former Stevens house in March 1955.

Violet Glenby bought in 1935 a 10-acre lot on the north side of Tinton Avenue from Judge Thomas Haight, hiring Nevius & Quackenbush of Shrewsbury to build this substantial Colonial Revival house. The architect is unknown, but Frank Quackenbush designed many of the firm's projects.

Edward Laurino founded Laurino Farms at 773 Sycamore Avenue in the 1950s. Children traipsing through the pumpkin patch in October best characterizes the place. Edward regarded them as "his kids," and became known as the "pumpkin man." He died in 1976, but the pumpkin tradition continues to this date.

Fred Wettach Jr., son of a Deal riding stable owner, bought 17 acres on the east side of Hope Road in December 1928, likely in anticipation of his elopement with Barbara Guggenheim. Barbara was a noted horsewoman, the daughter of Solomon, the noted art collector and museum founder, and granddaughter of Meyer Guggenheim, the renowned industrialist and summer resident of Long Branch. Their romance of riding culminated in marriage January 1, 1929; it was her second. The house, of Colonial Revival influence, was reportedly the first built on Hope Road, and is consistent with construction of the period. Little changed, it is now the primary division of Ranney School. (The Dorn's Collection.)

The 27-year-old Fred Wettach sold securities, but retired after marriage to build an equestrian estate. Its fine facilities included these large and commodious stables, a show ring, and a polo field. They named their place Trillora Farms. Fred was a champion jumper on horses, establishing world records in 1929 and 1930. The building, retaining the name the "Barn" as home to the lower school at Ranney, is easily recognizable today. (The Dorn's Collection.)

44

This picture of a second Trillora barn dates from 1948, as do the two on p. 44. The Wettachs underwent a "friendly" divorce in 1938, with Fred retaining the jumpers and the Tinton Falls estate, while Barbara kept the saddle horses. Russell G. Ranney bought the property in 1966 from later owners, for the Ranney School (pp. 80-1). (The Dorn's Collection.)

Hope Road is seen from the air *c.* 1950 showing the residential construction that filled the street in the 1930s and 1940s. (The Dorn's Collection.)

The 1954 opening of the Garden State Parkway ushered a building boon in the new borough. Shrewsbury Park, off Hope Road, was in close proximity to Fort Monmouth, appealing to their personnel, recalled original buyer Kay Welch, wife of officer Louis Welch, who was stationed there. They opted to retain their house even during his periods of distant assignment. Stratford Road is shown here looking south in 1955.

The typical Shrewsbury Park house was a 71-foot ranch designed by Turano-Gardner Architects, built on over one-half acre, which sold for $17,500. Their appeal to commuters claimed a one-hour trip to New York (although their ads did not state that trip was timed at 3:00 a.m.). This summer of 1955 picture shows 38 Stratford Road under construction.

The Shrewsbury Park houses were among the few in their price range that contained four bedrooms. The developers offered a "million dollar way of life," citing the proximity of famous stables (p. 44) and country gentleman farms (p. 121). This is a northern view of Stratford Road. The community has aged well and appears little changed, with its streets projecting to this viewer a mature quality development dating from a period of great growth in the area.

This June 1958 picture from 38 Stratford Road was taken looking toward Cloverdale Circle at the western reach of Shrewsbury Park. Ostensibly enjoying the swings, although that is not readily discernible from their expressions, are Louis C. "Chuck" Welch Jr. at left and his sister Joan.

This may be a 1930s image of the former Luke Conrow house on County Highway 537, near, and perhaps across, from the Colts Neck border. The house and a large farm were owned by Benjamin Wikoff and his son Frank. Later, in the 1920s, the property was sub-divided following its sale by Frank.

Del Brier Farms at the northwest corner of Sycamore and Hance Avenues, the latter visible in the upper right corner, has belonged to numerous notable owners, including the Hance family, which had extensive holdings in the area. Later the Thomas Secrest place, it was also owned by the noted prizefighter Mickey Walker, who inherited it from his mother. Both Secrest and Walker reportedly modernized the old house that now stands at 5 Linda Place, a new, post-development street. Jack Delaney, a New York restaurateur, bought the place from Walker in 1938. (The Dorn's Collection.)

Jack Delaney announced plans when he bought Del Brier to convert an old barn to a modern stable. Presumably it was this one, then located in the rear of the house, seen here in a mid-1950s picture. New housing now fills the site around the old farmhouse. The barn was presumably taken down during development. (The Dorn's Collection.)

Newman Springs Road, the northern border with Red Bank, runs near the top of this *c.* 1930s aerial. Pirates Stadium, earlier known as Oriole Park, is the clear space near the center shaped like, well, a stadium. The home of those two Red Bank teams was in Tinton Falls. Also visible are Hance Park houses and the Red Bank Airport. (The Dorn's Collection.)

In August 1951 Edward Berman bought the 10-acre Paramount Farm on the north side of Tinton Avenue. He made improvements, but discovered suddenly in March 1953 not only was he in the path of the planned Garden State Parkway, but the Highway Authority offer was, in his eyes, inadequate. (The Dorn's Collection.)

Berman made a vociferous and public protest claiming rough tactics were about to leave him homeless and in debt. He resisted selling, holding out for a better offer, with the sale to the Highway Authority finally effected June 30, 1954. Berman used the same Brooklyn address on both purchase and sale deeds, so presumably he had another residence. Both pictures are from March 1953. (The Dorn's Collection.)

George A. Steele, an Eatontown nurseryman, bought the 37-acre George Coleman farm on Tinton Avenue in 1910, intending to raise flowers and shrubs, and to use its site on a prominent road as a showplace for his business. The property once belonged to Abel Coleman, a prominent political figure; its house burned long prior to the 1910 transaction. This 1952 photograph shows the property at the northerly entrance to Branford Circle at a time when evergreens filled the plot.

The former Steele property was owned by Alston Beekman in 1954 when sold for development to the Branford Homes Company of Maplewood. A May 13, 1954 news item in the *Register* announced plans for 38 ranch-type houses in four models, each containing three bedrooms and 1 1/2 baths. This 1960 aerial shows all 38. The Parkway is at right; the Tinton Falls School is the large building at left. (The Dorn's Collection.)

This *c.* 1970 aerial embraces much of the former 200-acre George Hance Patterson farm. The Red Bank Airport is right of center, running between Shrewsbury Avenue at top and Hance Avenue at bottom. The latter street, earlier known as the "back road to Shrewsbury," was renamed by Patterson in 1923 when he divided the 60-acre section of his farm, left of center, into 40-by-120-foot lots for the Hance Park development. The streets are named Orchard and for popular varieties of fruit—Apple Street is the wider one left of the airport—giving rise to the facetious name "fruit bowl." The Tri Tac Building at the southeast corner of Hance and Apple no longer stands, but can be seen on p. 65.

This 1952 picture appears to be of the former Louis Steinmuller chicken farm on the west side of Tinton Avenue near the CECOM Building. The farm, which Steinmuller bought from Benjamin L. Atwater on January 1, 1930, had been owned prior to 1928 by Isadore Topchik, who reportedly built the chicken houses. New construction is on the site now.

Benjamin Beverly is seen in 1973 on his 10.5-acre pig farm on the north side of Hockhockson Road, Pine Brook. He bought the property with William Beaty as joint tenants that year, but died in 1976. Beaty sold to a developer in 1986 for the Regina Estate houses on the site now.

Joseph Patalano and Nicholas Castello bought about 40 acres on Water Street in 1922 as tenants in common. When the former acquired the latter's interest in 1928, he announced plans to divide it as small 5- to 10-acre small farms, but held the property into the 1940s. This Sears house was built presumably c. 1920s, but identification of the model is precluded by viewing only the side. The place still stands, now expanded, and is part of a nursery property.

John D. and Ella Crawford owned a summer home named "The Pines" and about 85 acres in southern Tinton Falls near Shafto and Shark River Roads. The house, heated but without a bathroom, was surrounded by a porch on three sides and was located near a hill from which Asbury Park was visible. The property, including the building that appeared to be of mid-19th century origin, was bought by the federal government in 1944 for part of the Earle Naval Ammunition Depot; the house was demolished.

Bill Anderson recalled that his first house at 1304 West Park Avenue was designed as a garage, but was suitable as a residence before his and Bea's family grew. Rather than expand this, they moved little more than across the street to a new house, built on the Ocean Township side of Green Grove Road. This house still stands, barely recognizable amidst considerable expansion.

The traditional house at 3515 Shafto Road was built in 1904 by Edgar White to replace one destroyed by fire that July 4th. The older building and farm were reported to have been in the Shafto family since the late 18th century. The place received the New Jersey Agricultural Society's Century Farm Award in 1979.

The former Shafto house at 115 Shark River Road, seen in 1981, is a large mid-19th-century house built in two sections. It is representative of the southern section neighborhood known as Shafto Corners, one with few visible reminders today.

Seabrook Village, begun by Senior Campus Living in 1997 on 134 acres with an address of 3000 Essex Road, is expected to be one of New Jersey's largest retirement communities. This view was taken in November 1998, only days after the first building opened in a complex with an announced completion total of 1,650 apartments for independent living, 192 assisted-living apartments, and 160 skilled nursing home beds. The Village, which expects to be able to provide varied levels of care through the aging process, has the potential to add about 2,600 residents to the borough's estimated population of 15,000.

Tinton Falls housing trends over the past ten years have embraced town houses, condominiums, large developments, and a southerly direction of the population center. Cambridge Park, built by V.S. Hovnanian, is among the more attractive developments. The long-term impact on voting patterns, traffic, and municipal services (notably education) will likely be profound, but, of course, can only be suggested in a work of history.

Three

BUSINESS

The Monmouth Consolidated Water Company's old Swimming River Reservoir on the Tinton Falls/Middletown border had a dam with an overflow line of 15.4 feet, a height overwhelmed by storms in 1955. Growth in the area also required greater capacity than its 200 million gallons, so a new dam was begun in 1958 and the reservoir enlarged. It had an overflow line with a 35-foot elevation and a reservoir designed to impound about 2 billion gallons. This picture is dated 1962, an aerial of a scene readily and most often viewed looking west while on the Swimming River Road Bridge. (The Dorn's Collection.)

The former hotel at 823 Green Grove Road, Wayside, had been known for many years as the Half Way House, so named as it was a stagecoach stop at the mid-point between Red Bank and Manasquan. It was built in 1846, according to Ellis' 1885 *History of Monmouth County*. James H. Dangler owned it from 1865 until discontinued it as a hotel in 1884. The site, now a private residence, is readily recognizable from this *c.* 1911 Alick Merriman photographic postcard. (Collection of Glenn Vogel.)

In the latter years of the 19th century John C. Crawford founded a slaughterhouse and wholesale meat business behind his home at 750 Tinton Avenue. This picture of a severe December 1947 snow storm may be the only surviving image of the slaughterhouse, at left. The smaller building was a garage. The business was discontinued with the 1965 retirement of his son Allen.

Wayside, a neighborhood now bisected by the Ocean Township border, was known as Centerville, probably from the late 1840s, and later as Danglertown. The latter name, from an owner of the hotel, may have been informal, not having been found on maps or primary sources. The name Wayside was adopted with the 1890 opening of a post office, in order to avoid confusion with another Centerville post office; the Wayside office closed in 1906. This *c.* 1911 Merriman photographic postcard shows the general store then owned by D. Battjer, with his three daughters seated on the porch. The place, located next to the Half Way House, was derelict for years before finally "collapsing," as one longtime resident recalled, perhaps *c.* 1940s. (Collection of Glenn Vogel.)

Linehan's Store, seen in 1952, sold candy, in addition to the liquid refreshments on the sign, making it a popular stop with students at the nearby Tinton Falls School. It occupied the southwest corner of Tinton Avenue and Water Street, and was demolished at an unspecified date; the site is now occupied by the Sunoco gasoline station. (The Dorn's Collection.)

Atlantic Superama, a major appliance dealer, is seen *c.* mid-1960s at 980 Shrewsbury Avenue, near its juncture with Highway 35. The building is today's Tinton Falls Plaza, occupied by many small shops. The building has been remodeled, with the brick corner, now stuccoed, providing a hint of recognition. Food City, which perhaps lived up to its name at the time, would be tiny by today's standards, but a 55,000-square-foot super market now adjoins, having opened in 1998. (The Dorn's Collection.)

Merco Enterprises was a Superama-licensed vendor. This 1965 picture of their department was only seven years into the long-playing record revolution; those platters are now as antiquated as the 78s they replaced. A linguistic cause of the author's suggests calling "CDs," records, an abbreviation for "recording," since compact discs now have supplanted LPs. Then the term "CD" can be reserved for certificates of deposit. Readers, look who is on the wall. You can say you saw Elvis hanging around. (The Dorn's Collection.)

Although the Dorn's negative envelope was marked "New Shrewsbury," the truck lettering and a business directory indicate Red Bank Custom Tire was on the Shrewsbury side (east) of Shrewsbury Avenue. Regardless, this is a fine 1953 image of a new business building of the period. (The Dorn's Collection.)

William A. Fluhr, a Red Bank Texaco distributor, joined his Vail Homes Service Station operators Joe Procano, left, and John Scorzelli on June 14, 1964. The station, located at 872 Shrewsbury Avenue on the Tinton Falls side of the border with Shrewsbury Borough, has not sold gas since the mid-1970s, but looks similar and is still allied to the industry as the German Auto Repair Shop. (The Dorn's Collection.)

Curvon Corp., founded in New York in 1891 for the manufacture of horse blankets, was bought by Harry Banta *c*. 1915. They moved to Red Bank in 1955, building this plant, designed by Harry's son John, at 34 Apple Street *c*. 1960. The handsome Colonial Revival-inspired facility, once the only business on the street, appears little changed, but was joined by much additional construction, and a side street, Hartford Drive, would now be on the left of this *c*. 1960 picture.

Curvon Corp. President John Banta, left, and Loris Clark, a foreman, are seen in 1967 holding a trophy blanket woven for the winner of a race, in this instance one at nearby Freehold Raceway. The firm also carries a line of baby blankets.

John Banta planted a row of trees behind his building to provide eventual shade and to serve as a barrier against the adjoining airport. An errant aircraft was running on the ground c. 1961, parallel to the trees, and struck one; the tree, contrary to the rational behind its planting, directed the plane into the building, damaging the structure.

The 33 Newman Springs Road location of Tinton Falls' first bank underscored development from north to south. Monmouth County National Bank built this branch in 1959 on the Red Bank border, on a street well-traveled by the 1954 opening of the Garden State Parkway and in proximity to business districts of Tinton Falls and adjoining towns. The building embraced the colonial motifs consistent with the organization, then headquartered in Freehold. This building still stands, part of First Union Bank, following several mergers. Tinton Falls State Bank has provided community-oriented banking since its 1980s opening, but it is also now part of a larger organization, Commerce Bank. (The Dorn's Collection.)

Daniel Dondi, born 1899 in New York, worked at several local restaurants prior to opening the Airport Inn in March 1937 on Shrewsbury Avenue, just north of Apple Street. He ended a 34-year tenure in 1971. The name was continued for a while, but the place was later converted to a pizzeria and is now a restaurant. The occasion of this November 18, 1963 visit of a horse-drawn surrey is not known; Dondi appears to be the one seated on the passenger's side. (The Dorn's Collection.)

Air View Inc. built the Red Bank Airport in 1926 on part of the George Hance Patterson farm, located between Shrewsbury and Hance Avenues. Apple Street is the wide thoroughfare running top to bottom at right. Jack Casey was aviator for the firm, which conducted an aerial photography business. An air taxi business that began in 1950 grew into a third level carrier, primarily taking passengers to larger airports. A number of accidents preceded the airport's closing in July 1971. Commercial development has been filling much of the airport grounds. (The Dorn's Collection.)

The Tri Tac Building at the southeast corner of Hance Avenue and Apple Street was dedicated August 18, 1967. Built for and leased to Fort Monmouth, the structure was also known as the Mallard Building as it housed the Mallard Project, a center of operations for an international task force developing field communications for the armies of the United States, Australia, and Canada. The building, faced with brick and gray-tinted glass, was demolished recently; its lot is now vacant (1998). (Historian, Fort Monmouth.)

Hope Road's 1975 paving between Highway 36 and Wyckoff Avenue permitted its development, including the construction of the five-story Hilton Inn on its west side, near the highway. The 120-room hotel, with restaurant, ballroom, and meeting rooms, was begun in 1975 and completed the next year.

Bowling enjoyed a great surge of popularity in the 1950s. Many bowling structures from that period now dot Monmouth County absent their lanes, including 800 Shrewsbury Avenue. The lines of the building, as seen in 1961, are readily identifiable, but one needs to view them from the side as the current occupant, an electric supply store, has a new, modern-style store built in front of the facade. (The Dorn's Collection.)

An elaborate ice skating rink suggested an enduring form of indoor recreation when built in 1974 off the west side of Shrewsbury Avenue. However, hockey had not yet attained its present popularity; business waned, and the facility closed.

Kenneth Granderson, left, is seen in May 1974 at his newly opened kennels, holding the first boarder. Sharing the moment at 2960 Shafto Road are three supporters—Victor Leiker, of Atlantic Highlands, representing the Service Corporation of Retired Executives; Granderson's banker, Richard Gaskill; and contractor William Johnson. The kennels, since expanded, are now the home of the Associated Humane Society.

M.J. Stavola, Inc. opened an asphalt plant on Hamilton Road, Pine Brook, in 1952, a time of great expansion of local paving activity. The proposals of early planners for the newly formed borough to expand Pine Brook as an industrial area in view of its locale along a rail route were rejected in order to preserve the area's residential character. The Stavola site, shown here in a recent photo, now includes an office building, built in 1979 facing Wayside Road.

The original *c.* 1900 photograph is labeled "Joe Cole and Alvin Shafto's team and bakery Wagon." The scene may be in the Shaftos Corner region in the southern section of the borough. However, the exact spot has not been determined and one wonders if Shafto's first name was actually Calvin. (Collection of Glenn Vogel.)

August Thomas operated an automobile repair garage in Asbury Park prior to buying land at the southeast corner of Asbury Avenue and Shafto Road in 1937, opening a gasoline station the following year. The plot needed 4 feet of fill to raise it to road level, which August accomplished himself, but the location was crucial as Asbury Avenue was a key feeder road to Asbury Park from Route 34, then one of the principal roads to the shore.

The construction of the Earle base closed a section of Asbury Avenue east of Route 34 (p. 123), but the Thomases expanded their business in the 1940s with a small restaurant and two cabins for tourists, seen at left. August took wartime employment at Raritan Arsenal, while his wife, Marie, known as Minnie, ran the business, seen here in the 1940s. She ran the business again after his death in 1951.

The Thomases built residential quarters over the garage and moved there in 1948. The garage was rented for a while, but Marie Thomas retained the gas pumps and operated what had become a local general store. Their sons, Fortune and Wayne, took over the business and today operate Thomas Brothers Auto Body Repair on the site. This picture is from the 1960s.

McDonald's, the most recognizable roadside icon of the second half of this century, attained leadership and status that permitted a style change in the 1970s from the streamlined golden arches structure to a discreet, modified Mansardesque building, such as this example at 588 Shrewsbury Avenue. It is seen near completion in July 1983, back in their 45 billion days. Today's competition for children's parties resulted in the construction of a large, box-like playground enclosure in front of the building. Imagine nostalgia for an "old" McDonald's in only 10 years!

Mini-storage is a major growth industry of the late 20th century. Hovnanian Enterprises' Hovpark, ten buildings with 593 rental units totaling 55,600 square feet, opened at 950 Shrewsbury Avenue in May 1982. Management appealed to the large number of renters in the area, but the mini-storage business is also spurred by Americans' proclivity to retain unneeded, even useless, possessions. Clutter costs, even if confined to our homes, but the author is not prepared to cast the first stone. Think about it and you may head to the nearest closet after putting this book down.

Four

SCHOOLS

Artist Evelyn Leavens, seated second from left, and her literary beagle "Boswell," whose *Boswell's Life of Boswell*, an illustrated volume quoting canine advice and observations apropos to humans, was a 1957 national bestseller, are seen at a June 1958 program to a New Shrewsbury class. Mingling with the students between the second and third rows near the left was the morning's second presenter, Alfred E. Neuman, who, upon learning he had the daunting task of following Boswell, responded with a characteristic, "What, me worry?"

The Wayside School, built 1856 on the west side of Hope Road, the border with Ocean Township, was one of three schools in Woodlands School District Number 79, according to the Wolverton 1889 *Atlas of Monmouth County*. It is now a private residence, having ceased instructional use at an unspecified time. The former school is seen on a *c*. 1910 A. Merriman photographic postcard. Since then, the porch was removed and the building expanded. (Collection of Glenn Vogel.)

A second Woodlands District school in Wayside was on the Ocean Township border on Green Grove Road. This apparent *c*. 1915 structure standing at number 721 is an unusual local example of a small brick structure. Its withdrawal from educational use is also unspecified. The building is now a private residence, its appearance improved from this 1981 view by removal of construction equipment, but obscured by maturing shrubs.

The origin of the Tinton Falls School is likely a small structure built in 1912 to replace a building destroyed by fire. Several additions were made, including one to its east side designed by Alexander Kellenyi and built c. 1935. The former entrance is believed to be illustrated in this undated picture. Note the former Methodist church at right.

The cast and stage of a Tinton Falls School class play are seen c. 1935. Wilma Crawford O'Callaghan, seated at left, recalled the students having made the sets and costumes, using a lot of crepe paper, with an artistically skilled boy painting the backdrops.

73

The Sycamore School was built in 1954 financed by federal funds as a replacement for a Vail Homes School annex. Its architects were Coffin and Coffin of New York and Victor W. Ronfeldt of New Shrewsbury. The building then had six classrooms, an all-purpose room, teachers rooms, and offices. It has been expanded repeatedly and was renamed for Mahala F. Atchison in 1973. (The Dorn's Collection.)

The federal government paid for a post-World War II addition to the Tinton Falls School to replace temporary classrooms built in the Vail Homes community building. This image, labeled by Dorn's "Tinton Falls School June 3, 1957," is presumably the village school, but, if so, it exhibits parts enveloped by later construction. (The Dorn's Collection.)

This October 10, 1957 picture of a school ground-breaking does not identify the site or subjects, although the date suggests the Swimming River School. The rapid construction of new housing that followed the 1954 opening of the Garden State Parkway strained the borough's system despite the expansion of the Tinton Falls School and construction of the Sycamore School. (The Dorn's Collection.)

Crowding forced the Tinton Falls system to double sessions by the time of the 1959–60 construction of the Swimming River School. It is set back west of Hance Road at number 220, out of view from the street. The school, seen in April 1960, then contained 12 classrooms, a kindergarten, an all-purpose room, and offices, but has been expanded since. (The Dorn's Collection.)

Mahala Field, who was born in Somerville, NJ, and received her undergraduate education at Cheney State, PA, began her teaching career in Cedar Hill, MD, in 1925, coming to Monmouth County to teach grades one through eight in the one-room segregated Pine Brook School. Following its c. 1943 closing, she taught kindergarten at the Vail Homes School, where she is seen with her 1949 class. Mary Nimitz and Lois Berry are in the first row, center and right respectively, while Claire Thomas Garland, lender of the picture, is at right in the second row.

Field earned graduate degrees, studying at several universities. She later taught first grade at the Sycamore School. In 1950 she married the Rev. Wallace William Atchison. She is shown here overseeing a tug-of-war at the spring 1972 field day at the Sycamore School, which was later renamed in her honor. Eugene Welsh is the boy second from the left.

Mahala Field Atchison was a member of numerous educational and spiritual organizations and received many awards. She was a lifelong member of St. Thomas AME Zion Church in Pine Brook. Atchison retired in 1973 after a 46-year career teaching in Tinton Falls. Not long after, the Sycamore School was renamed in her honor. She is seen in September 1983 when a portrait in her honor was hung in the hall of that school. Patricia Schleig, right, president of the PTA, is pinning the corsage. Atchison died in April 1985.

The origin of the Pine Brook School, at left, is unclear. The structure shown on the 1889 *Wolverton Atlas* was located some distance from the Hamilton Road location in this 1944 picture. The school closed *c.* 1943. M. Kenneth Taylor Sr., born in 1928, was a career postal worker, scout leader, community activist, and choir member of St. Thomas. He married Mildred Christian, had eight children, and died in 1965. The Pine Brook Community Hose Company (p. 107) is now on the site.

George C. Malone, born around 1911, was for many years the Tinton Falls superintendent of schools, and is seen in 1974 as he contemplated retirement. The 1934 Colgate graduate had various New Jersey teaching positions prior to his appointment as supervising principal in Tinton Falls in 1949. The system of about 500 students and 16 teachers expanded rapidly early in his tenure. Malone claimed their greatest accomplishments were complete integration of the system, initiating one of Monmouth County's first child study teams for the cognitively impaired, and obtaining considerable federal aid (reflecting the presence of Vail Homes in the system).

The "original bell from the first Tinton Falls school" was unveiled November 20, 1974, in the hall of the present building in honor of longtime superintendent of schools George C. Malone, second from the left, seen receiving congratulations from his successor, Dr. John F. Fanning. Mrs. Malone is next to the bell, while Mrs. Marvin Sims, president of the PTA, is at right.

The Tinton Falls School library was dedicated on December 8, 1971, to the memory of V. LaDonna Peck, who, as school librarian for 12 years, was known as a friend of the students and for her single-minded dedication in establishing the library. Her husband, George Peck (right), is seen presenting a painting by their son Paul in her honor. Accepting it are Keith Olson, president of the Tinton Falls Board of Education, and Mrs. Ivan Kaminow, librarian.

Carol Garvey, chair of the playground development committee for the Mahala F. Atchison School, is seen in July 1975 with her daughter Allison, looking at a model of recreation equipment to be built with parent-volunteer assistance. Carol, a registered nurse, still lives in the borough with her husband, Eugene, a former councilman. Their two other children are Mary and Gerard.

Russell Gaylord Ranney, a World War II veteran educated at New York University, founded a private college preparatory school at his Rumson home in 1960. He served as Tinton Falls Supervising Principal from 1946 to 1949 and was active elsewhere in establishing programs focusing on the importance of reading in education. The school purchased an extensive tract on the east side of Hope Road from Mildred Tufano in April 1966, an amalgamation of properties that included the Wettach Trillora Horse Farm. This *c.* 1980 aerial shows new Ranney construction, but also reflects the campus' agrarian origins. (Collection of the Ranney School.)

The Student Commons Building, begun in 1986 as an expansion of a farm structure, opened in the spring of 1987. It contains a bookstore, music room, and student lounge on the first floor and lunch, kitchen, and assembly facilities on the second. Closed walkways connect the Commons with the high school and barn buildings. (Collection of the Ranney School.)

The lagging of athletics behind the strong academic programs at Ranney was addressed by the 1975 construction of a gymnasium, a multiple phase project that also embraced new classrooms. Russell G. Ranney at right and Mayor Gabriel E. Spector are wielding the shovels at the May 13th ground-breaking. Also present, from left, were Donna Baldino, senior class president; Cathy Daniels, student council president; Ian Horne, architect; and Herbert Hand, builder.

The new athletic facility, the Brod Building, is seen in December 1977. Today its facade is hardly changed, other than by the inclusion of identifying letters, along with a sign indicating it as "home of the Panthers." The building is named for William Brod, a Ranney parent and c. 1970s board member. The complex, also housing the middle school, consists of two similar brick buildings connected by the natatorium, which contains a fine swimming pool and other athletic facilities.

The June 1955 graduating class is seen outside the Tinton Falls School. The principal, George C. Malone, is in the center of the first row, while two teachers, Elizabeth Conover and Frances Ottinger, left and right respectively, flank the middle row. Ruth G. Borden preserved the picture; she is in front, sixth from the left.

Students at the Tinton Falls School are seen in March 1976 exhibiting one of their bicentennial projects.

Five
ORGANIZATIONS

The Newman Springs area, on today's border with Red Bank, was sufficiently isolated from the settled part of that town in 1893 to be chosen for the site of a quarantine hospital during that year's smallpox epidemic. The one-and-one-half-story structure appears to be the 24-by-60-foot hospital building reported to have contained a superintendent's office at one end, with the remainder divided by a hall separating ward rooms. The two-and-one-half-story building is likely the staff's residence. Other buildings on the premises included a laundry/store room and a wagon shed. (Collection of Robert S. Osborn.)

The history of the Methodist Episcopal Church at Tinton Falls is vague. They may have organized *c*. 1815, were apparently incorporated *c*. 1834, and had an early church that was rebuilt in 1872 and rededicated in 1873. This edifice, seen in 1952, was located north of the Tinton Falls School, which owned the building prior to its removal *c*. 1961 for an expansion of the school. (Collection of Robert S. Osborn.)

The St. Thomas AME Zion Church, the present name of the congregation founded in 1854 as the Macedonian AME Zion Church, is located on the southwest corner of Squankum and Hamilton Roads, having been relocated from its original Water Street location. The original 1884 Gothic Revival building substantially rebuilt *c*. 1931 following extensive fire damage; it has unusual aluminum board and batten siding. The sign denotes them as the "friendly church at the crossroads where everyone is welcome."

The Roman Catholic Church of St. Anselm was established in 1972 and created from parts of several parishes in nearby towns. Mass was first celebrated at the Wayside School and then at a parish house purchased in June 1972 at 6 Pine Lane, Ocean Township. The present church at 1028 Wayside Road was built in 1974 on Diocese of Trenton-owned land, which was once considered a potential cemetery site. Its architect was parishioner Charles G. Surmonte, whose plan reflected new guidelines of the Catholic bishops that churches be designed to reflect a climate of hospitality.

St. Anselm's was expanded in 1992, also to Surmonte's design. The new space is at right in this interior view taken from the rear of the sanctuary. The non-traditional space is dramatic and moving, reflecting the architect's intent that the surroundings encourage worshippers to be involved as participants rather than as spectators. The feeling of the interior is suggested by its warm wood finishing, the high, irregular ceiling lines, and its seating surrounding the altar platform. The congregation is known for its warm, caring spirit and its community involvement, including a strong social action program.

The Monmouth Reformed Temple was organized in 1959, initially meeting for eight years at the Shrewsbury Presbyterian Church. This synagogue at 332 Hance Road, designed by Rodetsky-Siegel of Freehold and dedicated in 1967, is seen in 1984. Expansions include an education wing in 1977; an enlargement of the sanctuary and social hall in 1988; and the addition of a second floor in 1998, designed by James J. Monteforte of Neptune.

Rabbi Sally Preisand, born 1947 in Cleveland, OH, was the first woman ordained a rabbi in the United States. She was educated at Hebrew Union College in Cincinnati, where she completed a five year program in four years. Preisand's early career included seven years as an assistant rabbi at the Stephen Wise Free Synagogue in New York and two years as rabbi at Temple Beth-El in Elizabeth, NJ. She came to the Monmouth Reformed Temple as rabbi in 1981, the date of this picture in her office. She continues to hold her position there. She is also president of Interfaith Neighbors.

Sid Martin's major sculptural work was large, blown fiberglass pieces, often inspired by the theater, in active or contemplative poses. The Middletown resident was a longtime exhibitor at the Monmouth Festival of the Arts at the Reformed Temple, an annual exhibit founded in 1971. *Comedy*, a double-sided work— *Tragedy* is on the reverse—is seen on exhibit there in 1993. For years it was mounted at the entrance to the artist's home street, White Oak Ridge Road in the Lincroft section, prior to being sold to a collector following the artist's death in 1996. The exhibit that year had a Monet theme, exemplified by Elizabeth Alsina's attire as the title character from *Linnea in Monet's Garden*.

The Monmouth Church of Christ had its origins in the early 1940s, when a few Fort Monmouth personnel sought others to worship in their tradition, meeting at various locations. Red Bank and Eatontown groups in time met at a purchased synagogue and church respectively. They merged and in 1968 built this edifice at 312 Hance Avenue, designed by Shrewsbury architect Gerard A. Barba. The church has assumed a strong posture in community service and is home to a number of organizations.

A Dutch Reformed congregation was formed in Red Bank in 1902. In time they acquired the earlier Grace Methodist Church at Shrewsbury Avenue and Leonard Street, later expanding and remodeling it. They occupied that building until 1956, when they built this 40-by-80-foot edifice at 62 Hance Avenue, designed by John T. Simpson, Red Bank architect. (The Dorn's Collection.)

The First Presbyterian Church, Eatontown, was founded in 1927. It was later renamed the Hope Presbyterian Church in 1985 and moved to a new structure at 1189 Hope Road in 1994, designed by parishioner Charles Dunn, working with the office of architect James Mancuso. The tower contains stained glass that embraces symbolic images of the Jesse tree prophesy (Chapter 11 of Isaiah), designed by Suzanne Mahns. Those images, now executed in glass by the Keegan Studios, became a memorial to Mahns.

The Reeveytown AME Zion Church was founded *c.* 1880, building this structure at 3023 Shafto Road *c.* late 19th century. The building was rebuilt following fires in 1954 and 1969. However, it was sold to Monmouth County for the expansion of the nearby reclamation center and was demolished in 1994. A new edifice built nearby was completed near the time of this book's publication.

In 1979 the Tinton Falls Citizens Committee and the Tinton Falls Veterans Association protested a proposal to build a sludge composting plant behind the Reeveytown AME Zion Church on Shafto Road. They claimed the process of using wood chips to filter sewage sludge had potential environmental hazards. Citizen protest was a factor in the plant not being built.

Monmouth County acquired a major tract on the west side of Shafto Road in the Reeveytown section for construction of a recycling center and sanitary landfill in the 1970s. This construction scene dates January 1975.

The buildings pictured above are seen nearing completion in July 1975.

The center has two buildings containing shredders, such as this 1,000-horsepower example. Processing also removes ferrous metals. Inspecting the facility in July 1975 were county officials, from left to right, Freeholder Ernest G. Kavalek, Planning Director Robert D. Halsey, and Freeholders Thomas J. Lynch and Harry Larrison Jr.

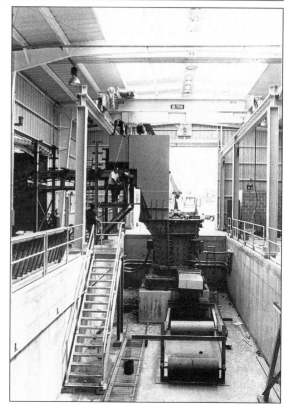

This second view of the shredder building is also dated July 1975. The success of the recycling ethic brought an unanticipated problem. Since it costs more to operate the center than its recycled products yield in revenue, the county suspended recycling operations in October 1998.

Max Phillips bought about 275 acres of the Peach Blossom farm c. 1929, which spanned the Tinton Falls and Eatontown border, planning a first-rate housing development and country club. A clubhouse and golf course were built on the Eatontown side, while the Tinton Falls sector included a polo field and two artistic houses. (p. 121). The Monmouth County Country Club Racing Association conveyed about 200 acres to the Philrush Realty Corporation in 1940; they, in turn, sold the property to the federal government in 1942, which expanded Fort Monmouth by establishing Camp Charles Wood. (Historian, Fort Monmouth.)

A signal research and development laboratory was begun in 1953 to centralize work performed in four locations. Initially known as Building 2700, the structure would be named Myer Hall, but is widely known as the Hexagon. A second section was built in 1953, resulting in the shape reflected in this c. 1960s picture and its appearance today. The final two sides were not built. A structure later erected at Fort Huachuca, AZ, appears to be the missing piece. Local lore claims that base received the final segment "belonging" to the Hexagon. (Historian, Fort Monmouth.)

This 1970s aerial shows at left a portion of the Hexagon building, a chapel, and a since-demolished movie theater, but its principal interest is the SCEL Field Lab #2, the Eatontown Signal Lab, in front, built in 1942 primarily for aviation electronics. After World War II, the building was the site of the Air Force's Watson Labs and the Army avionics lab now known as the CECOM Electronics Integration Directorate. (Historian, Fort Monmouth.)

The Army formerly maintained a training ground in a wooded area around Wayside, the site of this c. late 1940s photograph of exercises by the 497th Signal Photo Service Company. The precise spot of this scene in a facility that embraced Eatontown and Ocean Township land, in addition to a Tinton Falls section, is not known. At that time the Army contemplated a possible major expansion of its holdings in the area, but dropped them when Signal Corp training facilities were moved out of state. (Historian, Fort Monmouth.)

The Dworman Building Corporation built at Tinton Avenue and Wayside Road a six-story office of over 700,000 square feet in 1972–73 for lease to the Army's Electronics Command. The structure, seen in November 1972, was notable as the borough's largest tax ratable, for its 3,000-car parking lot, and for its dismal aesthetics. Its cladding is aluminum. Work spaces were small, creating a large population for its size, which created massive traffic at rush hours.

The CECOM Building became its new name following an Army reorganization of Communication-Electronic Command units that resulted in the transfer of Philadelphia personnel to Fort Monmouth. Army employment there waned in recent years, ending in 1998, the year the building was sold to buyers planning a remodeling to Class A office space, including new exterior cladding. The Camp Charles Wood area of Fort Monmouth is at the upper right, while Branford Circle housing is above the building at center in this 1973 photograph. (Historian, Fort Monmouth.)

In 1943, the Navy, seeking a new weapons storage and shipping depot distant from a population center and the congestion of New York Harbor, bought extensive tracts in Middletown, Colts Neck, Howell, and Shrewsbury Townships. The facility, initially an ammunition depot, was later elevated to a Naval Weapons Station, and was named for Rear Admiral Ralph Earle, chief of the Bureau of Naval Ordnance in World War I. The embankments in this 1953 photograph were built in what would become Tinton Falls as protection for the overnight storage of loaded railroad cars. Present practice is to load and unload quickly, avoiding such storage. (Official United States Navy photograph.)

Normandy Road, the Earle connection from the inland base to its pier in Leonardo, Middletown Township, has a short stem in Tinton Falls from the Swimming River border with Middletown to Swimming River Road, a crossing that remained at grade. The public struggle that ensued over crossings resulted in overpasses at busier intersections, including nearby County Highway 537 in Colts Neck and the state highways. (Official United States Navy photograph.)

The Tinton Falls Borough Hall was once owned by Peter Casler, who built a 28-foot square house in 1894, attaching it to an older structure. His farm of about 87 acres, containing a fine apple orchard, was sold to Jesse Cornell in 1917. This view was taken in 1966. A parking lot has since been built in front and a police extension added on the east, or left. (The Dorn's Collection.)

The importance of the falls as a local symbol as well as a major feature of the county's physical geography is represented in this mural by resident Dorian Cleavenger, seen in an October 1975 presentation to the borough. From left to right are Councilwoman Ellen Branin, William A. Barrett, local historian, and Mayor Gabriel E. Spector.

A measure to end the confusion of the Borough of New Shrewsbury with tiny, but ancient, Shrewsbury Township and the venerable Borough of Shrewsbury, was taken by voters on November 4, 1975. They approved a public question on the election ballot by a margin of 1,069 to 745 to change the municipality's name to the Borough of Tinton Falls. Some areas opposed the change, including the Shafto Road and northeast districts. Artist Bill Canfield was ready with a sketch symbolizing the new name; the drawing was accepted by Mayor Gabriel E. Spector.

The borough council passed on November 6 a resolution officially changing the municipal name to Tinton Falls. Mayor Gabriel E. Spector is seen signing the resolution. At left is Dale H. Shick, council president and Jerome S. Reed, borough clerk. Reed recalled that his mother, Margretta, witnessed a related historic event. She was the borough clerk when New Shrewsbury was formed from Shrewsbury Township in 1950.

The municipal name was different at the January 1, 1976 government reorganization meeting, but the faces were the same. Present, from left to right, are as follows: (seated) Council President Dale H. Shick, Mayor Gabriel E. Spector, and Ellen Branin; (standing) Arthur E. James, Irving Cohen, Walter J. Trillhouse, and Elizabeth Q. Billings. James and Billings were reelected in November 1975; the others were holdovers. The government adopted the Mayor-Council Plan under the Optional Municipal Charter Law on July 1, 1985.

Ann Y. McNamara, mayor of Tinton Falls in 1998, has served in that office since 1989, but began public service about 30 years earlier in roles that include volunteer librarian and activist with the League of Women Voters. Municipal positions date from her 1976 appointment as an alternative to the zoning board. A native of Watertown, MA, the mother of five was honored as the 1998 Eastern Monmouth Area Chamber of Commerce's Elected Official of the Year. Her recent accomplishments include negotiating a manageable agreement on solid waste facilities and contributions to the rebuilding of the bridge in the village. Ann is seen in a 1978 photograph.

The Tinton Falls Public Library occupies the *c.* 1930s Craftsman-style Silas Cronk house at 664 Tinton Avenue. Cronk, a former Shrewsbury Township justice of the peace, built a 30-by-20-foot living room that also served for his official duties. William Placek, its second residential owner, built an extension in 1956 and sold the place to the borough in 1976. The library was founded in 1961 and initially occupied a rear room in the former Methodist church (p. 84) then used for a school storage building. It later relocated to the borough hall on Tinton Avenue. This 1978 image still reflects a residential character.

The library, containing 23,000 books, was officially opened on Sunday, February 13, 1977. Present at the dedication were, from left to right, Councilman Irving Cohen, Library Association President Eric Holmgren, and Borough Council Member Arthur James.

Officer Gatchel "Tootie" McCall is seen at the Bicentennial Parade in 1976. The borough made a decision not to change immediately all manifestations of the old name. Eight months after Tinton Falls was adopted, his vehicle still sported the New Shrewsbury designation, which appeared to be wearing off. Eugene Welch is the boy holding the banner.

Patrolman Al Van Hauter is at the wheel of the first police car to bear the borough's new insignia, designed by borough resident-artist Thomas Ruzicka. The sycamore leaf suggested life, the vigor of growth, and the open character of the town, while its three segments represent the falls and the municipality's three names. The flattened circle is symbolic of unity. At left is Police Director Walter Dodwell with Mayor Gabriel E. Spector.

An official gathering appears proud of the borough's new GMC garbage truck in 1956. (The Dorn's Collection.)

The Tinton Falls municipal dump opened *c.* early 1950s on the west side of Hope Road, then a rough, unpaved path, and closed *c.* late 1970s. The site is near the United Parcel Service building and the Route 18 exit ramp. Bottle diggers beware! You would not want a piece of highway overpass falling on your project.

Tinton Falls Fire Company Number 1, once aligned with the Ocean Township system, incorporated in 1934, and bought from William Bennett in 1938 the lot that contained the old, presumably original firehouse at the southeast corner of Tinton and Sycamore Avenues. It is seen in 1952. Note the platform-mounted signal bell, which was re-installed nearby at ground level as part of a firemen's memorial. (Collection Robert S. Osborn.)

The Tinton Falls Fire Company bought an additional lot from Russell Peterson in 1948. Their members built this firehouse in 1954–55 to replace the structure pictured at top, locating it in front of the old building. Labor was provided by company and local volunteers, while materials were largely donated, with some paid for through a "Dollar for a Block" fund drive. The flat-roofed, concrete floor building measured 30 by 36 feet, with its three bays accommodating their three pieces of apparatus. The picture appears to date from near its 1955 completion.

Members of the Tinton Falls Fire Company again employed self-help to erect new quarters. They hired artisans for the footings and pavement, but performed much of the construction labor themselves, as evidenced in this view of their work on the framing in January 1982.

Personnel of the Tinton Falls Fire Company appear to be pleased, *c.* 1954, upon receiving a new Mack fire truck. The three who are identified are, second from the left, Al McMoyle; Clarence Unterbert, an elected official; and George O'Callaghan, chief that year.

The Wayside Community Fire Company, founded in 1919, was encouraged and supported by the Wayside Women's Club. The company initially used a variety of second-hand, non-motorized equipment, including Indian tanks strapped to the firefighters' backs. The tanks were helpful in fighting brush fires, the principal activity in their early years in the then-sparsely settled neighborhood. Such fire fighting gave rise to the company's nickname of the "Stump Jumpers." Their insignia—this example is a patch—was drawn by Bea Anderson, wife of fireman Bill, c. 1950. In recent versions the firemen added the figure of a bee in her honor. (With thanks to Stephen Grabley.)

The Wayside Community Fire Company built the two-story frame firehouse at left c. 1922 at the triangular juncture of Green Grove and Wayside Roads, on the Tinton Falls side of the border with Ocean Township. The present one-story brick firehouse was built in 1964, but the old one was retained for meeting rooms. The two are pictured in 1975, when the company was engaged in a fund-raising campaign to add the present meeting rooms to the north side of the building. The old firehouse was later demolished.

The Wayside Community Fire Company's early motorized equipment typically consisted of used vehicles adapted by the members for fire-fighting purposes, including a Model-T Ford, a Dodge, a Studebaker, and a Packard. Bill Anderson, lender of this *c.* 1930s photograph, does not recall which it is, other than it is "not the Dodge." The first man on the left remains unidentified; the others are, from left to right, Clarence Brocklebank, Al Dangler, and Joe Dangler.

In 1950 the Borough of New Shrewsbury purchased two Ford F8 fire trucks with 145-horsepower motors and the capability to pump 500 gallons per minute at 120 pounds of pressure. They are seen in February 1951, shortly after the arrival of the Wayside vehicle, which followed several weeks after the Tinton Falls truck was delivered. (The Dorn's Collection)

Jack Casey was known to have begun advertising by air, dropping circulars from a plane in 1920. The means were more sophisticated by decade's end, as evidenced by the Ford Trimotor at top and center, photographed August 24, 1929, with product listings painted on the plane. The caffeine content of the beverages at top suggest the advertising slogan "You'll fly high with Monarch in the morning." The man with the tie in the center photograph appears to be Casey. The August 30, 1929 image at bottom shows the first light, then newly installed at the airport.

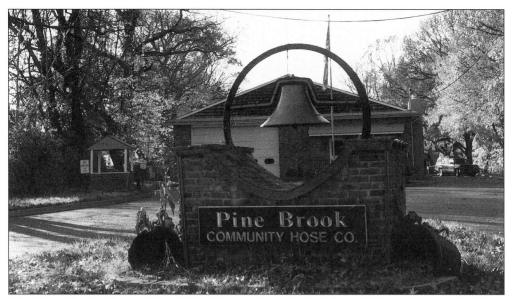

The Pine Brook Community Hose Company was founded c. 1941, occupying their first firehouse on Hamilton Road near the railroad tracks. The present firehouse at 70 Hamilton Road, the former site of the Pine Brook School, was begun in 1945 and expanded later.

The Pine Brook Community Hose Company grew accustomed to a variety of used equipment, so the purchase of their first new fire truck in 1965 was a time of special pride. Visiting the Ford plant in Detroit to pick-up the vehicle, which was driven back to New Jersey, were, from left to right, as follows: (bottom) Milton Reevey, Charles Leonard, and Oliver Jackson; (standing) unidentified, Bill Leonard, and Clayborn Butts.

The Monmouth County Mosquito Control Commission operated from their headquarters at 143A Wayside Road.

The Wayside Grange met at the local firehouse, the site of this c. 1940s unidentified gathering. Seated fourth from the left with the white hat is Jeanette Cobb. Walter Cobb Sr., her husband, is to her right, while Marie and Walter Cobb Jr. are to her left. George and Bessie White are standing to the right of the flag.

The Monmouth County Organization for Social Service used funds from the Louise C. Bodman Foundation to build this regional center in 1958 at 1100 Wayside Road, seen here *c.* 1958, naming the building for her. A health center of the time was an office and equipment facility for their visiting nurses. The building, later headquarters for the organization's hospice program, is now the Bodman Regional Center, home of clinical specialists of the Visiting Nurse Association of Central Jersey, the name MCOSS adopted in 1994. (The Dorn's Collection.)

The Association of Retarded Citizens, known as ARC, is a not-for-profit organization educating and assisting those with mental and physical needs. Their home at 1158 Wayside Road includes the Dorothy B. Hersh High School. The facade facing west was built in 1990. ARC activities include a variety of workshops, recreation, employment opportunities, and group home services.

Troop 94 of the Boy Scouts of America was sponsored by the Pine Brook Community Hose Company. These Boy Scouts, seen at an unidentified *c.* 1945 event, are, from left to right, as follows: (front) Leroy Wingo and Gerald Deveaux; (back) William Greenhow, Wilfred Jones, Ernest Reevey, Ludwell Ashton, and Jerome Deveaux.

The Pine Brook Scouts had a flag used on ceremonial occasions. Seen at its presentation at a 1963 event are, from left to right, Milton Reevey, an unidentified member of the scout council from Oakhurst, Oliver Jackson, Scoutmaster M. Kenneth Taylor, Bill Leonard, and Joseph Mickens Sr. The troop has not been active since the 1965 death of Scoutmaster Taylor.

Six

PEOPLE, PLACES, AND EVENTS

The Tinton Falls Fire Company's *c.* 1932 minstrel show featured this pack of handsome and lovely revelers. The mock wedding "joined" John Lemon and William Pillis—the latter was the bride. An array of period women's fashions are portrayed. However, look carefully; those are no ladies sporting them. Some females are pictured; most are wearing ties. The taste quotient may be low by contemporary standards, but this is the way people enjoyed themselves as recently as a generation ago.

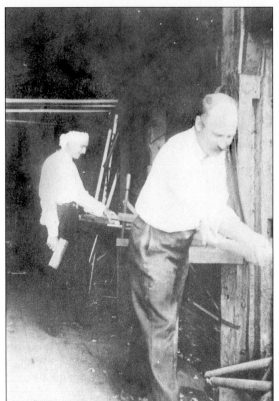

Thomas W. Walling, foreground, an aviation enthusiast, and his brother Peter, a civil engineer, built an airplane in David A. Walling's blacksmith shop in 1910. Tom received patents for a stabilizer, a balancing device shaped like an elongated walking beam, which was intended to keep the airplane stable while in flight. Perhaps they were tinkerers more than inventors, as no record was found of successful flight. Tom built a number of tested models from 1908 to 1910, but awaited the return of his brother from a South American gold mining expedition before beginning his major work. The engine and propeller were purchased, but the rest of the craft was built in the shop. (Collection of Richard C. Winters.)

Flight stabilization was a major pre-occupation of avaitionists of the time. Early airplanes had multiple wings; this monoplane design was new. The wing span and length were 36 and 24 feet respectively. Its Elbridge engine developed about 40 horsepower with the 600-pound craft expected to have a lifting capacity of 1,000 to 1,200 pounds. The photograph is dated 1910. (Collection of Richard C. Winters.)

Building the airplane was a costly project, reaching perhaps $5,000 per one press account, exclusive of the Wallings' time. The brothers hoped to attain commercial manufacture capability. Thomas Walling sold off pieces of his farm and even his horse (presumably the one he rode in on) to pay the project's expenses. He sold stock with an authorized capital of $200,000, but subscriptions, primarily from family and neighbors, were no doubt far less. Note the incorporation in Arizona two years prior to statehood. One can infer the territory was likely the wild west of securities regulation. (Collection of Richard C. Winters.)

"Tinton Falls Will Soar to More Fame" read the headline of the New York *Globe and Commercial Advertizer*, on November 8, 1910, of a story also reported in the local press. Unfortunately, no record of flight has been found, nor has one been passed in family lore. One present resident's father recalled seeing the plane tethered to the ground, its storage condition to prevent flight during motor testing. But did it attain sustained flight? Evidence was not found by the time this book went to press, and the author, ordinarily loathe to repeat rumor, suspects that only a brief, minor lift off the ground was attained. (Collection of Richard C. Winters.)

The fair in early September was a town tradition for many years, with its beauty contest a prime feature. At top left is Debbie Ross, who was the last to earn the title Miss New Shrewsbury in 1975. Three winners following the name change to Tinton Falls are, clockwise from upper right, Joe Ellen Noland, 1979; Jennifer Tarantolo, 1985; and Georgia Marie Gross, 1981. Each earned the distinction at age 16. The multi-talented Joe Ellen also sounds good, now enjoying a career in communications doing voice-overs.

The Pine Brook Cemetery is seen in October 1978 when Raymond Peterson of Boy Scout Troop 100 organized a clean-up campaign. Samuel Teicher, left, supervisor of Veterans Internment of Monmouth County, and Scoutmaster Robert Klenk, right, review the work. The site received another cleaning in 1998, demonstrating that cemeteries need not only large project overhauls, but on-going care and maintenance.

The Wayside Fire Company organized an annual excursion to Coney Island, NY, in its early years; some traveled on a fire truck. Seen there, perhaps in the 1920s, in front of a painted backdrop, are, from left to right, as follows: (front) Hamilton Truax, Lynn Osborn, Harold Pitcher, and Harold Connors; (back) unidentified, Dave Osborn, Joe Dangler, unidentified, Clarence Brocklebank, and Al Dangler.

Joseph Richardson is pictured with his wife, Anna Theodora, and their children *c.* 1900. They are Julian Russell Richardson, between the two, and in the rear, from left to right, Christina, Leona, Ryers, and Charlotte. The Richardson clan and the Revey family (also spelled Reevey) include descendants of the Cherokee (who migrated in the 1780s from the Cherokee Nation in Georgia) and local Lenapes. Their extensive property in the Sand Hill/Richardson Heights area was initially in Shrewsbury Township, but municipal division has left much of it in the Neptune Township area near the southern sector of Tinton Falls. There has been extensive intermarriage between African Americans and the group known as the Sand Hill Indians.

The Indian Council of the Sand Hill band of the Cherokee Nation is seen at their 1949 meeting, probably at Richardson Heights. From left to right are as follows: (seated) Theodora Richardson Bell, Edith Richardson Gardner, Christina Richardson Dickerson, Adeline Richardson Thomas (grandmother of Claire Thomas Garland), Restolla Richardson, and Charlotte Richardson; (standing) James Lone Bear Revey, Jonathan Richardson, Isaac Richardson, Chief Ryers Crummel, Robert Richardson, and Robert Revey.

Left: The Thomas children, shown here *c.* 1915, are, from left to right, Allen, Madeline, and August. The latter built the Reeveytown Servicenter seen on p. 69. *Right*: The three daughters of Nita and Herman Morris of Reeveytown are, from left to right, Hermanita, Romana, and Renee. Herman, a cousin of August Thomas and a descendent of Ryers Crummel, believed that photographs took part of one's spirit—a superstition that was once apparently held by a number of Native Americans—so pictures of the Morris family are rare.

Family ties are strong and reunions have always been a favored means of maintaining them in Native-American and African-American communities. Isaac R. Richardson and Elizabeth S. Revey married in 1844. Some of their descendants gathered in Tinton Falls for a 1980 reunion. They include Claire Thomas Garland, kneeling at right, and her brother, August Thomas, standing fourth from the right. August is a former educator and retired administrative law judge. The third woman from the left in the middle row is Ida Morris, a daughter of Herman and Nita, and a granddaughter of Ryers Crummel.

Riverdale Avenue was split into two sections by the 1953 construction of the Garden State Parkway, with the resultant segments designated "east" and "west." A large quantity of earth from the Riverdale area was sold to grade slopes elsewhere on the Tinton Falls segment of the project. The street is viewed at an unspecified point in May of that year.

Earth moving in the Tinton Falls area began around early May 1953. This September picture shows the beginning of the construction of the Sycamore Avenue Bridge.

Major progress on the Sycamore Avenue Bridge was made by December 1953. The existing curve of Sycamore Avenue at the overpass suggests how the bridge was built next to the former roadway.

The Sycamore Avenue Bridge became a favored spot for viewing traffic, especially at peak conditions. This view is Memorial Day, 1976. Traffic was moving then, although many will recall bumper-to-bumper vehicles, notably proceeding north on summer Sunday evenings.

West Park Avenue was in the heart of downtown Wayside when Alick Merriman took this *c*. 1911 photograph looking east for a postcard. The Half Way House is at left, while the border with Ocean Township is in the background at the Hope Road intersection. The Wayside locality predated the 1849 separation of Ocean from Shrewsbury Township. Its bisection by a municipality change created the expected opportunities for confusion.

Sycamore Avenue looking east at Hope Road is seen in 1981 with a large, white cross, a symbol that provided a target for aerial photographers. The county was "re-mapped" that year, with the photographs used for a variety of planning and zoning purposes. Some crosses can still be seen around the county, but this busy intersection's mark was effaced following re-paving, the installation of a signal light, and the repainting of traffic lines.

Tinton Avenue looking west at Hope Road looked remote and rural in 1961. The corner, part of the border with Eatontown, was changed markedly with the *c.* 1980 construction of the Lenape Woods condominiums, the installation of a signal light, and the expansion of traffic lanes. The character of the residences on the north side of Tinton Avenue, unseen beyond the trees, is little changed, however. (The Dorn's Collection.)

Tinton Avenue's eastern stem looking east is the straight road up and down this *c.* 1950 aerial, a thoroughfare historically known as the Eatontown-Freehold Road, or Turnpike. The northern side became Gentlemen's Farms *c.* 1930s, while the southern side, after a spell as country clubs, became the Charles Wood area of Fort Monmouth. Below the golf course, Hope Road is the border with Eatontown. Lafetras Brook is the border near the northeast corner of that intersection, so the north side of Tinton Avenue east of Hope Road is in Eatontown. The entrance to Monmouth Regional High School is now near the lower left corner, while the borough hall property would be below the picture at right. (Electronics and Communications Museum, Fort Monmouth.)

The juncture of Swimming River Road, right, with the county highway, now known as Route 537, was long a key Tinton Falls intersection and is a border with Colts Neck Township. The top photograph was likely taken a year or two prior to the middle one, early in the 20th century. Roads alternately sandy and muddy were long a major county public works issue. A rural character was still present in the early 1950s scene at bottom. The billboards are gone, with the one in the center having a nostalgic interest for the pictured Miss Rheingold. The intersection, for many years one of the borough's most dangerous, was reconfigured c. 1995 with turning lanes, and a new signal light was installed.

Dick Winters is behind the wheel of this earth mover, ready for serious work on the Garden State Parkway. (Collection of Richard C. Winters.)

Asbury Avenue is an east-west road that intersected with Highway 34 at today's entrance to the Earle Naval Weapons Station. Prior to the base's absorbing a key section of the avenue, it was a major access road to Asbury Park; it now terminates abruptly west of Shafto Avenue. The scene is notably stark, given the infrequency on New Jersey roads of security fences, guard posts, and flashing red lights.

Wilda Bennett, born in 1894 to the prominent Monmouth County family, was Allen E. Crawford's cousin and a noted figure of the musical theater. She married four times, once to Long Branch riding instructor Anthony J. Wettach. She was publicly identified as the "spouse" of another man, a relationship that became the subject of an alienation of affection case in the 1920s. Wilda made her New York stage debut as Conscience in *Everyman* in 1911. She died in Nevada in 1967, the widow of her fourth husband, Munro Whitmore.

Maria Harrington operated a school of dance on the second floor of the village mill. Several of her students are seen at a recital in the Tinton Falls School *c.* early 1960s. The girl in profile at the far left remains unidentified, but the others are, from left to right, Joan Welch Castello, Carlyn Ewald, and Barbara Wilhelm.

Monmouth Memorial Park was founded c. 1930 to provide a burial estate, a place of beauty amidst nature without the presence of tombstones. Its Highway 33 location is often identified with surrounding towns, but it is nearly on the southern boundary of the borough. This c. 1930 picture shows the singing fountain and waterfall.

Site identification was to be marked with 12-by-24-inch bronze memorial plaques in order to preserve the park-like appearance of the grounds. The founders took special note of an elevation of more than 100 feet above sea level, despite close proximity to the shore. This picture, published c. 1930, is of the lower lake with hills in the background.

Genevieve Ridner made her first dollhouse c. late 1960s after finding local stores lacked what her daughter wanted. Captivated by the process despite a "primitive" first effort, she undertook serious study of the miniaturist's art, becoming highly skilled as she advanced to more complicated buildings and detailed projects. The Tinton Falls resident took some of her greatest inspiration in nearby Shrewsbury, where her great, large-scale models of the Presbyterian and Christ churches and the Allen House are on exhibit at the Shrewsbury Historical Society's museum. Her output's less serious side included realistic models of diners. Gen is pictured with a 1976 project.

The Swimming River Garden Club planted a spruce tree in November 1976 in the village green as a memorial to Wilda Sidoric, a past president of the club and a member of the borough Shade Tree Commission. Councilwoman Betty Billings is kneeling; standing, from left to right, are club members Mary Boeglen, Alberta Strimaitis, and Mary Cain. The latter two were also past presidents.

The pre-World War II expansion of Fort Monmouth required housing for their growing number of personnel. The federal government purchased a tract on Shrewsbury Avenue for construction of Vail Homes, a project that would have a profound impact on rural Shrewsbury Township. The contours on this *c.* 1980 aerial view compare readily with the "Red Bank B & L" tract at the right of the map on p. 2, at the curve of Shrewsbury Avenue. The first houses were completed in 1941 for occupancy by soldiers and their families. The enclave expanded in the early war years, built around three streets. (Collection of the Ranney School.)

The late 1940s population of the .09-square-mile Vail Homes was nearly the same as the remaining 15 square miles of Shrewsbury Township. Vail residents were government renters, but had equal voice in raising and expending municipal tax funds. They achieved the dubious distinction of "representation without taxation." The balance of the township addressed this specter by separate municipal incorporation as a borough, effectively "divorcing" Vail Homes, leaving that housing project (which the government later sold) as the sole remainder of the once-vast township established in 1693. (The Dorn's Collection.)

The New Jersey Division of Fish, Game, and Shellfisheries long-raised game birds and mammals for stocking hunting areas. Most pheasants were raised on their farms at Rockport, Warren County, and Forked River, Ocean County. The division's John Bahn is seen in November 1978 releasing some of that year's 8,000 pheasants on open land in the Tinton Falls area.

A goat is the author's signature closing, although one can not be found for every town and this one is not in the preferred pose in front of a cart. Thus, the handsome fellow, an apparent winner of a pet contest at the 1954 New Shrewsbury Fair, the borough's second, will have to be imagined as preparing for a victory lap, pulling its proud owner. (The Dorn's Collection.)